CHURCH UNIQUE
[VISUAL SUMMARY]

Copyright 2010 Will Mancini, All Rights reserved
NOT TO BE REPRODUCED
without express written consent from Will Mancini
ISBN-13: 978-1468171471
ISBN-10: 146817147X

the story behind the
[VISUAL SUMMARY]

"When I wrote Church Unique, I was creating a field manual based on my vision work and missional coaching with church leaders.

Over time I realized that it was entirely possible to miss an important concept or tool in the book due to its comprehensive approach. Therefore I wanted to help existing readers see everything that it contains in a more accessible and engaging way.

Some people even critiqued the book as being too complex for a book on simplicity. For those people I have two responses.

First, it's simple to make things complex, but its complex to make things simple. If there is complexity in the book, the complexity serves to make a life of vision simple in the end.

Second, because I love the idea of synthesis, I did want to share the entire book with very few words—one hundred and eleven to be exact. I hope that brings an elegant summary to those who felt understandably overwhelmed by the longer field manual."

- Will Mancini

the [VISUAL SUMMARY] flows in four movements

[PART 1] Rethink Vision
Church leaders must reconsider the practice of vision today.

[PART 2] Uncover Uniqueness
Vision begins with a clear identity that reveals what your church can do best.

[PART 3] Talk Up Vision
Missional vision will answer five fundamental questions in a clear, concise and compelling way.

[PART 4] Live Out Vision
Vision is realized only to the extent that it is integrated into the life of the church, one conversation at a time.

[PART 1] rethink vision

Church leaders must reconsider the practice of vision today.

God's infinite creativity is so big it's mind-blowing. And you are a one-of-a-kind leader called in a one-of-a kind way. So churches, by design, are unique.

But pastors are copycats albeit unintentionally. Therefore, the concept of vision is caged, the practice of imagination is buried and our leadership talk is cheap.

As a result, our people are stuck in the small worlds of church that we create.

1234

God is big [and...]

GOD IS BIG

God's infinite creativity is boundless and His artistic genius is endless.

Snowflakes. No two are alike.
Sunsets. Each is it's own.
You. No one replicates anyone.

God doesn't use a photocopier.

you are called

In a place where image is everything, Rich Kannwischer guides a church that reveals the good life from the inside out.

Bruce Miller is called to start a multiplying network of people helping people find and follow Christ in the rural landscape of Northeast Texas.

Doug Kyle leads a group of creative relational cultivators, in a community that was devastated by forest fires.

...God is big and you are called [so...]

"For when David had served God's purpose in his own generation..."
— Luke (Acts 13:36)

"Here am I. Send me!"
— Isaiah (Isaiah 6:8b)

"I have brought you glory on earth by completing the work you gave me to do"
— Jesus (John 17:4)

"In the life of faith each person discovers all the elements of a unique and original adventure. We are prevented from following in one another's footsteps and are called to an incomparable association with Christ. The Bible makes it clear that every time there is a story of faith, it is completely original. God's creative genius is endless. He never, fatigued and unable to maintain the rigors of creativity, resorts to mass-producing copies."
— Eugene Peterson

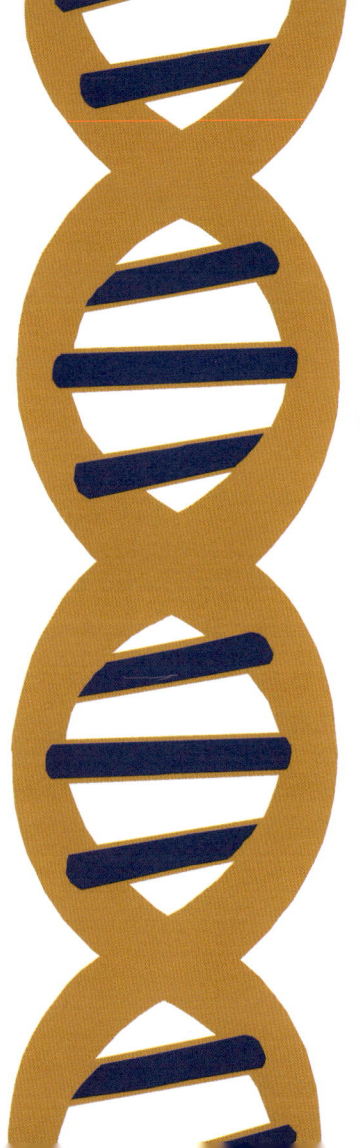

...you are called, so churches are unique [but...]

CHURCHES ARE UNIQUE

The differences between congregations are becoming greater with the passage of time. The safe assumption today is that no two are alike. Each congregation has it's own culture.
— **Lyle Schaller**

Each congregation plays the music a bit differently, even if it plays the same piece as the group down the street, the music emerges uniquely because the musicians are not the same. Smart conductors discover the sound within their band and exploit it. Wise church leaders do so as well.
— **Max Lucado**

Each band of Christ followers is one-of-a-kind.

pastors are copycats

...churches are unique, but, pastors are copycats [therefore...]

It's easier to duplicate than incarnate. Therefore, most ministry leaders miss what God is up to.

Unoriginal Sin = copycat models
Incarnation = design your own model

Unoriginal Sin = cut and paste language
Incarnation = put it in your own words

Unoriginal Sin = impotence by cloning
Incarnation = vitality through birth

...pastors are copycats, therefore, vision is caged [because...]

STATEMENTS GOALS TAGLINES STRATEGIC PLANNING NOTEBOOKS OBJECTIVES PRIORITIES METRICS

VISION IS CAGED

When did we forget that vision transfers through people *NOT* paper?

Without vibrant imagination, vision gets caged and called something that its really not. **We use lots of different words to get at this thing called "vision."**

"Changes that appear turbulent to organizations that rely heavily on planning may appear normal to, even welcomed by, those who prefer a more visionary or learning approach. Put more boldly, if you have no vision but only formal plans, then every unpredicted change in the environment makes you feel like the sky is falling."
— Henry Mintzberg

Introducing the *Thinkhole*.

...Vision is caged because imagination is buried [and...]

Ministry Treadmill...No time to think
Competency Trap...No need to think
Needs-Based Slippery Slope......Needs are all we think about
Cultural Whirlpool ...... **BuzzChurch:** Addicted to new thinking
Cultural Whirlpool .... **StuckChurch:** Too tired to think
The Conference Maze.......................Let's borrow their thinking
Denomination Rut ....No one helps us think

IMAGINATION IS BURIED

" We make fully devoted followers of Christ. "
– The Everyday Pastor

" Our five purposes are worship, fellowship, evangelism, ministry, and mission. "
– The Everyday Pastor

" Our vision is to love God and love others. "
– The Everyday Pastor

...imagination is buried and **talk is cheap** [so...]

TALK IS CHEAP

...talk is cheap, so people are stuck.

people are stuck

The real reason people call your church home is probably one of four reasons. The truth is that these are a little disappointing.

1. Place – We make our buildings and then our buildings make us. People get addicted to space unless the space serves a bigger vision.

2. Personality – 15-35% of your people are most deeply connected to your church because of a pastor or staff member.

3. Programs – Just try to shut one down. It's hard to change when our people get their identity from how we do things instead of why we do things.

4. People – Many call your church home because they know a handful of people who sit near them or attend a class together. It's easy to rely entirely on the comfort food of community without cause.

Question: What is your unique calling as a church, that transcends place, personality, programs and people?

[rethink vision]
the story behind this icon

A pumpkin farmer was strolling through his rows of beautiful green leaves. At the beginning of the season, the acorn size pumpkins were beginning to add dots to the landscape. When he glanced down he noticed a clear glass jar and curiosity got the best of him. He brought the jar over to one of his pumpkin buds, slipped the small pumpkin inside and left it sitting there in the field. Months later, with the experiment long forgotten, the farmer walked his land with great satisfaction as large beautiful pumpkins covered the patch. Startled, he noticed the glass jar totally intact, yet completely filled up with that little pumpkin that grew inside. It was hard not to notice how the thin glass barrier defined the shape of the orange mass within. The pumpkin was only one-third of the size it should have been.

The problem for this little pumpkin is the same problem for most churches today. Rather than growing to their full potential based on their unique DNA, they conform to the shape of external molds or models. These "glass jars" create invisible barriers for growth and predetermine the shape of community for churches across the country.

Part one showed us the jars we need to break so that we can celebrate the organic, God-given shape and culture for each local church and, most importantly, your local church. Visionary leadership today seems to be about more "jar-sharing" than about DNA-discovering. Therefore, it's time to redeem vision by recasting it. We must rethink what it means to be visionary- to see it in a different light. Missional leaders can "break the mold" one church at a time by leading their people into God's unparalleled future for their church.

[PART 2] uncover uniqueness

Vision begins with a clear identity that reveals what your church can do best.

Clarity isn't everything, but it changes everything. Yet, clarity is rare in leadership because the chaos of process is required to achieve it. Clarity is worth it. It creates simplicity, which is beautiful to experience. It creates focus, which is amazing when you sustain it. Clarity enables movement. Movement is waiting for you and is God's plan for His people.

Since Jesus is clear and the legacy of the saints is speaking, let's get clear now for ourselves. There is so much at stake!

Clarity starts singular. Many leaders articulate an over-generalized sense of vision that is not singular. Your unique singularity is not "glorifying God" or "making disciples." Why not? God's glory is the ultimate motive for any church and discipleship is every church's Jesus-given mission.

So what's your singularity? What's your church's unique part in the Kingdom? We call that unique part your Kingdom Concept. How would you fill in the blank, [our church] exists to glorify God and make disciples by _____ _____.

1 2 3 4

Clarity changes everything [but...]

Clarity isn't everything, but it changes everything. *Clarity makes...*

- Uniqueness Undeniable
- Direction Unquestionable
- Enthusiasm Transferable
- Convictions Tangible
- Work Meaningful
- Synergy Possible
- Success Definable
- Focus Sustainable
- Leadership Credible
- Uncertainty Approachable

...clarity changes everything, but, chaos is required [yet...]

CHAOS IS REQUIRED

Like a diamond, clarity is forged, not formed. It takes time, heat and pressure.

We call it the tunnel of chaos...
Seth Godin calls it the dip....
St. John of the Cross called it the cloud of unknowing...

Don't be afraid to unmake, undo, and rethink. You'll be glad you did.

Pastors spend more time on sermon prep in one month than they do on big picture clarity in 5 years.

" Simplicity is the ultimate sophistication."
– Leonardo DaVinci

" When the solution is most simple, God is answering."
– Albert Einstein

" Less is more."
– Ludwig Mies van der Rohe

" I wouldn't give a fig for simplicity this side of complexity, but I would give my life for simplicity on the other side."
– Oliver Wendall Holmes

...chaos is required, yet, simplicity is beautiful [and...]

SIMPLICITY IS BEAUTIFUL

FOCUS
IS AMAZING

...simplicity is beautiful and, focus is amazing [because...]

Many churches struggle with clarity because their effectiveness bears more fruit. In other words, with success come more options. Ironically, these new options can dilute the very success that brought them. The key then is to uncover which opportunities are really distractions in disguise so they can be avoided or turned down. The ongoing irony is that more focus brings even more success, making it then again harder to maintain clear focus. Only those who sustain a single-minded resolve can continue to reap the hundredfold fruit.

The reality is that focus expands.

...focus is amazing because, movement is waiting.

movement is waiting

> " I wrote this book for one purpose— to challenge you to find your Church Unique— that is, to live a vision that creates a stunningly unique, movement-oriented church. "
>
> – Will Mancini

JESUS IS ~~confusing~~ CLEAR

Jesus is clear [and...]

"I have made known to you everything I heard from my Father."
– John 15:15

His greatest sermon can be read in eight minutes. (Matthew 5-7)

He summarized prayer in five phrases. (Matthew 6:9-13)

He silenced accusers with one challenge. (John 8:7)

He rescued a soul with one sentence. (Luke 23:43)

He summarized the Law in three verses. (Mark 12:29-31)

He reduced all his teaching to one command. (John 15:12)

He made his point and went home.
– Max Lucado

Since the time of Jesus, predecessors, mentors, peers and co-laborers across the globe work in response to the same revealed Scripture to usher in a better future on their own street corner. The question is, "How do past and present vision connect to what God is calling us to do?"

Seeing our vision as a single domino in the history of world redemption will simultaneously:

- Motivate us
- Humble us
- Sharpen us

...Jesus is clear and legacy is speaking [so...]

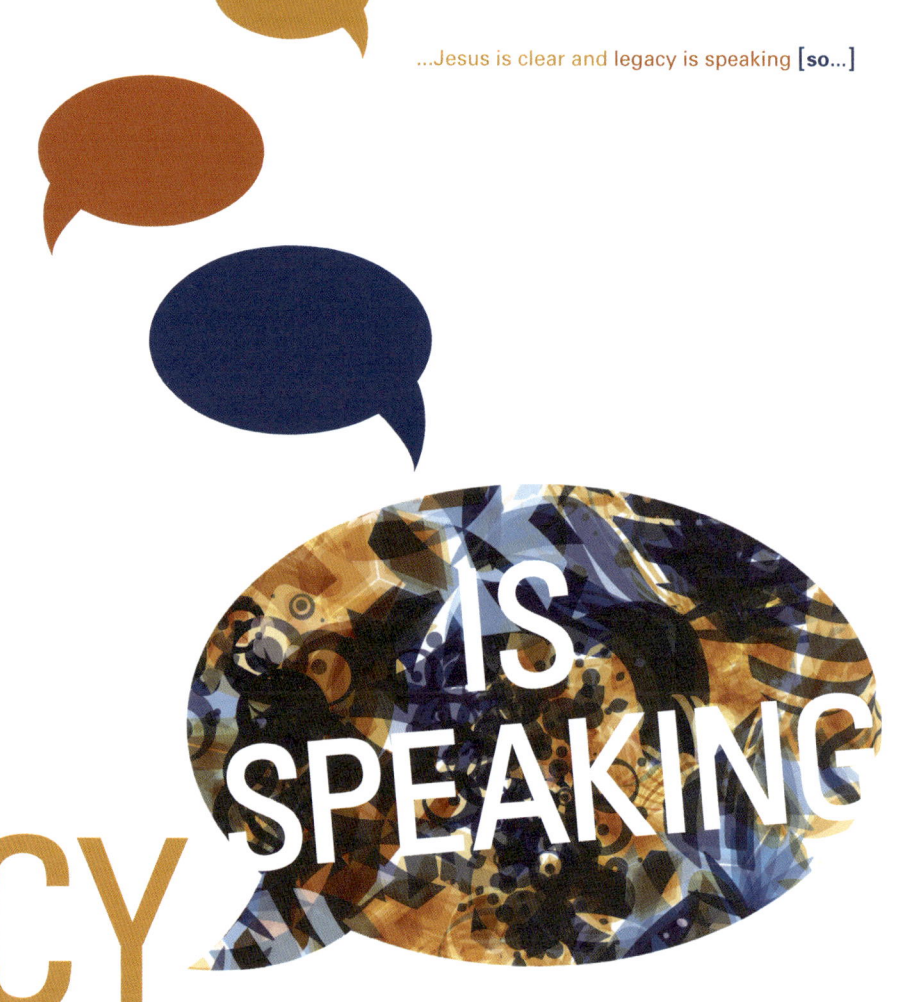

LEGACY IS SPEAKING

In prepping to get clear...

#1 Frame it first.
State your vision framework before you frame your vision statement. *Repent of stabbing at the future.* Be honest about whether you have enough clarity. If you only have a phrase or two that defines your future, that's not enough. What else do you need?

#2 Listen until you glisten.
Discern the future by seeing what you already have. *Repent of neglecting the obvious.* Ask more questions to those around you. Your team. Your congregation. Respected voices outside of your church. Do they think you are clear? What do they think is most important to the future?

#3 Team the horses.
Go farther by pulling together. *Repent from trying to do it yourself.* Collaborate, and call participants to pray together, dream together, and truly speak into the vision.

#4 Work outside in.
Discover an angel by inviting a stranger. *Repent the myth of objectivity.* Having a "strategic outsider" is a critical element. The greatest performers in any arena are so because they demand coaching.

...legacy is speaking, so get clear now.

GET CLEAR NOW

1 clarity starts singular

The universe contains "uni" because even the largest things have a singularity and a unifying essence

Every sermon should have singular idea. This singular idea is more specific than glorifying God and making disciples.

Every book of the bible has a singular message. The singular idea is more specific than glorifying God and making disciples.

Every church has a defining strength. This defining strength is more specific than glorifying God and making disciples.

We call your church's singularity your "Kingdom Concept."

...clarity starts singular, while glory is ultimate [and...]

GLORY
IS ULTIMATE

Glorifying God is ultimate, in that it should be our highest motive. Yet the idea of glorifying God is not a statement of vision.

In fact, everything really glorifies God in the end doesn't it? You will glorify God some day. When the righteous are saved God is glorified. When the unrighteous are judged, God is glorified. **The question is, "Will you choose now, His glory, as your highest motive?"**

The church was given a mission from Christ. This mission is rooted in the very character of God. In fact it's most accurate to say, **"The church of God does not have a mission, the mission of God has a church."**

This same mission, to "go therefore and make disciples" is articulated in unique ways according to context.

(Matt. 28:19, Mark 16:15, Acts 1:8, John 20:21)

DISCIPLESHIP IS GIVEN

...glory is ultimate and discipleship is given [so...]

Local Predicament
What are the unique needs an opportunities where God has placed us?

Collective Potential
What are the unique resources and capabilities that God brings together in us?

WHAT'S YOUR PART?

Apostolic Esprit
What particular focus most energizes and animates our leadership?

...discipleship is given, so what's your part?

What can your church do better than 10,000 others?

What is your great permission within the great commission?

What does your church uniquely bring to the Kingdom?

The Kingdom Concept is the overlap of three circles and completes the sentence, "Our church exists to glorify God and make disciples by _____."

[uncover uniqueness]
will's field notes

"...building a community of spirit-filled servants by fusing challenging teaching with environments of acceptance, diversity, wholeness and healing."
- Good Shepherd

"...bringing the whole gospel to busy young dads who have moved back to the city."
- Neartown Church

"...being ambassadors of grace to those burned by legalism."
- Grace Crossing

"...making belief in Jesus real in a make believe world."
- a Church in process

"...creating a center of arts and ideas from a Christian perspective."
- Presbyterian Church in a college town

"...turning everyday contacts (corporate rolodex, tall steeple, mission center contacts, relationship with community gov't) into spiritual conduits for God's power to transform almost Christians to altogether Christians."
- St. Andrew UMC

[PART 3] talk up vision

Missional vision will answer five fundamental questions in a clear, concise and compelling way.

Missional leaders frame up clarity by answering five irreducible questions. [What? Why? How? When? Where?] The Vision Frame is a tool to help you and your team solve the puzzle of vision clarity. There are four sides to articulate first.

- You must use a compass and answer "What we are doing?"
- You must light a fire and answer "Why are we doing it?"
- You must show the way and answer "How are we doing it?"
- You must hit the bullseye and answer "When are we successful?"

The fifth aspect of clarity is not another side of the frame—it's what you see in the middle. We call this Vision Proper. Vision Proper answers, "Where is God taking us?"

To be visionary you must dream a little "in the middle" of the frame. Then you can paint with words a lot— giving people a travel brochure for where God is taking you. Think "mountaintop view." Finally, you should mark your steps so that people push themselves and celebrate progress together. Think "milestone goal."

1 2 3 4

Frame up clarity [and...]

frame up clarity

There are five irreducible questions of clarity. Imagine every leader in your church being able to answer these in a clear, concise, compelling way.

1. **What are we doing?**
2. **Why are we doing it?**
3. **How are we doing it?**
4. **When are we successful?**
5. **Where is God taking us?**

Ideally, no leader should lead, no team should meet, and no initiative should start without a clear understanding of the Vision Frame.

...Frame up clarity, and **solve the puzzle** **[and...]**

Where do you start when you put together a puzzle?

The sides.

The Vision Frame is a tool to help you and your team solve the puzzle of vision clarity. It's a visual reminder of the five irreducible questions.

The first side of the frame is mission.

...solve a puzzle and use a compass [and...]

mis·sion –noun
a clear and concise statement that describes what your church is ultimately supposed to be doing.

The mission is your compass. It's your guiding north star. It's the holy orders for your congregation. It's the golden thread that weaves through every idea, conversation, and action, no matter how small.

Missional leaders embrace mission as the missional mandate (*ᵐMandate*) that Christ gave to the church.

Mission answers the question, "What are we doing?"

use a COMPASS

...use a compass and light a fire **[and...]**

light a FIRE

The second side of the frame is values.

val·ues *–noun*
shared convictions that guide the actions and reveal the strengths of the church.

Values light a fire. They are the common heartbeat of the church. They reflect your collective soul, your corporate grace. Values are filters for decision making and springboards for daily action. Think of values not as what we do, but as what characterizes everything we do.

Missional leaders embrace values as missional motives (*ᵐMotives*).

Values answer the question, "Why are we doing it?"

The third side of the frame is strategy.

...light a fire and show the way [and...]

strat·e·gy –noun
the process or picture that shows how the church will accomplish the mission on the broadest level.

Strategy shows the way. It's the rhythm of your church body. It's the pattern of participation. Strategy is your congregation's operational logic. Clear strategy helps you do fewer things with better quality so your people can do less church activity and live more for Jesus.

Missional leaders embrace strategy as missional map (*mMap*).

Strategy answers the question, "How are we doing it?"

...show the way and hit the bullseye [then...]

hit the BULLSEYE

The fourth side of the frame is mission measures.

meas·ures –*noun*
the attributes or characteristics in the life of the individual that reflect the accomplishment of the mission.

If you don't know what you are aiming for you can't hit the bullseye. The problem is that most churches only measure the ABCs: attendance, buildings and cash. But a circus can have good ABCs. What makes your church different than a circus?

Disciples. What kind of disciple is your church designed to produce? What is your church's portrait of a mature believer?

Missional leaders embrace measures as missional life-marks (*mMarks*).

Measures answer the question, "When are we successful?"

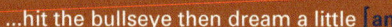
...hit the bullseye then dream a little [and...]

dream a little

Once the sides of the frame are complete it's much easier to discern and "see" what's in the middle. The middle is what we call Vision Proper. Vision Proper answers the question, "Where is God taking us?"

vis·ion pro·per –*noun*
the living language that illustrates and anticipates God's better future.

Think of Vision Proper as the travel brochure of the next destination that God has for your church. Use the four sides of your Vision Frame to help discern where God is leading you.

- Emphasize mission to regain redemptive passion
- Highlight strategy to increase involvement
- Choose a value to "heat-up" the culture
- Use a measure to strengthen spiritual formation

What is the single most important emphasis for the coming year? Pray and discuss this as a team. Believe that God will guide you. Choose to Focus. Decide together.

...dream a little and paint a lot [and...]

Once you know generally where God wants you to go, start to "paint" a specific picture with words. Imagine that you have the ability to create a breathtaking mountaintop view of your church's future. Then, imagine people responding with bold risk-taking, energetic collaboration, and heroic sacrifice.

If you want that kind of response, your specific vision picture will need to have six elements. Think of these elements as six colors that your "painting with words" will need to utilize.

We teach the six elements with the Vision Casting Spider Diagram to use as a preparation and evaluative tool.

1. Common denominator
2. Burning Platform
3. Golden Tomorrow
4. Wake-up Call
5. Mind Stretch
6. God Smile

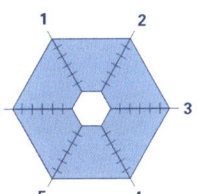

paint a lot

...discipleship is given, so **mark your steps**.

> *Don't give us a scorecard with five or ten or twenty metrics on it. Don't take all the metrics your organization can generate and present [them] a "balanced scorecard"...complexity confuses us and makes us anxious. It saps our strength and undermines our confidence...If you want us to follow you into the future you must cut through its complexity and give us one metric, one number to track our progress.*
> – Marcus Buckingham

There is one more thing to include with Vision Proper. In addition to the qualitative aspect of vision, you want a quantitative part. The quantitative aspect forces you to get really specific and provides a compelling thrust that your picture alone doesn't have.

Stay with one thing. Pick a date. Select a clear, measurable goal based on your single emphasis. Your people need to feel and celebrate progress. We call this your missional milestone. That completes Vision Proper.

Vision Proper = ^{m}Mountaintop + ^{m}Milestone

mark your steps

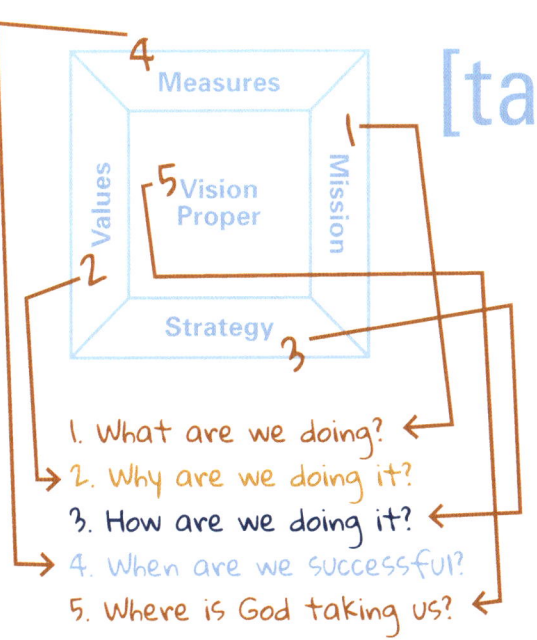

[PART 4] live out vision

Vision is realized only to the extent that it is integrated into the life of the church, one conversation at a time.

Movement is made not with great vision casting alone, but with small, ever-present steps of integration. Integration begins with people's hearts. Through dialogue, the soft stuff of attitudes, feelings, and expectations attunes. Integration includes the nuts and bolts of organizational life. Through decision-making the hard stuff of systems, structure, and communication aligns. Church leaders must learn to let "positive no's" work. Then leaders will bring people aboard the vision.

Don't stop talking about the Vision Frame until everything is integrated. There are five important areas of integration that transcend the typical silos of ministry.

Keep working at the vision God gives you. Trust in Jesus as your Lord and Savior and Chief Visionary. Don't stop believing that God dreams big.

1234

Movement is made not with great vision casting alone, but with small, ever-present steps of integration. **Integration is not a glamorous idea but it creates fabulous results.**

"Here's how Lyle Schaller once said it:
The crucial issue [for growth] is not the central theme of the strategy [for the church]. The crucial question is whether the congregation, including the configuration of the paid staff, is organized to be supportive of a clearly defined and widely supported central strategy."

Integration requires patience for dialogue, ingenuity in decision-making, and fortitude to use the "positive no."

Movement is made [as...]

MOVEMENT IS MADE

soft stuff attunes [and...]

Debates: Someone loses
Discussions: Someone dominates
Dialogue: Everyone wins.

"Dia" means with or through. "Logos" means word or meaning. Dia-logos is when peoples' streams of thought commingle to raise the waterline of awareness, understanding and meaning.

Integration of vision begins by harmonizing people's hearts. Through dialogue, the soft stuff of attitudes, feelings and expectations attunes.

Attune before you align.

soft stuff attunes

...soft stuff attunes and **hard stuff aligns.**

Integrating the hard stuff of systems, structure, and communication requires constant alignment.

It's all about persistent modification.

What can you...
- combine?
- subtract?
- double?
- adapt?
- reduce?
- reinvent?
- cage?
- tweak?
- add?
- eliminate?
- amplify?
- modify?
- cut?
- accelerate?
- concentrate?
- stop?

hard stuff aligns

"POSITIVE NO'S" WORK

"Positive no's" work [to...]

If you can't say "no" your vision won't go.

In a world of endless opportunity the word "no" is an essential tool for integration.

Think of your vision as the ultimate Yes. That Yes cannot live without lots of No's to guard it and protect it. A No that protects the ultimate Yes is a "positive No."

> It's easier to say No with a deeper Yes burning inside.
> – Steven Covey

> The right No is not the opposite of love but comes from love and grows toward love.
> – William Ury

> But when you enter a town and are not welcomed, go into its streets and say, 'Even the dust of your town we wipe from our feet...'
> – Jesus instructing his seventy-two person core team

..."positive no's" work to bring people aboard.

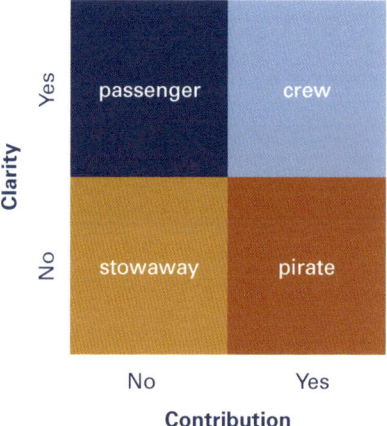

There are four kinds of people in your church when it comes to vision.

Passengers to nurture and challenge
Crew members to equip and empower
Stowaways to find and convert
Pirates to confront and eliminate

Don't stop talking [until...]

don't stop talking

Vision dripping is more important than vision casting.

Turn the practice of vision into a team sport. Imagine scores of people who can drip vision into every conversation and ministry decision in a clear, concise and compelling way.

Take your cue from the postman and deliver vision daily. Share your vision dripping idea on twitter with #visiondrip and join the cause of open source vision casting.

...don't stop talking until everything is integrated.]

everything is integrated

Integration creates new patterns for organic growth.

The enemy to integration is "business as usual" expressed in each of the churches "default" ministry areas.

Stop accepting and excusing the status quo.

Create new conversations in each ministry area until the Vision Frame is abundantly clear. The Vision Integration Model is a simple conversation starting point. Each component of the model transcends the typical silos of church ministry.

How are we integrating vision into:
- Developing leadership?
- Intentional communication?
- Duplicatable process?
- Compelling environments?
- Conscious culture?

Don't stop believing [that...]

DON'T STOP
believing

" It may be that the day of judgment will dawn tomorrow. In that case, we shall gladly stop working for a better future. But not before. "

– Dietrich Bonhoeffer

[live out vision]
your Vision Pathway notes

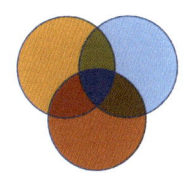

Our church exists to glorify God and make disciples by:

Mission:

Values:

Measures:

Strategy:

Mountaintop:

Milestones:

I hope you enjoyed the

[VISUAL SUMMARY]

My one request:
Draw the Vision Frame on a whiteboard and have conversations to answer the five irreducible questions of clarity. I invite you to check out these resources if you are interested in walking the Vision Pathway as a team. You can:

do it yourself – Church Unique Vision Kit | churchunique.com
join a coaching network – Vision co::Labs | auxano.com
journey with us, side-by-side – On-site Consulting | auxano.com

e-mail me: will@churchunique.com

come by my blog: willmancini.com

twitter: willmancini

Made in the USA
Lexington, KY
29 October 2014